SEÁN McGRAIL

ANCIENT BOATS AND SHIPS

Second edition

SHIRE ARCHAEOLOGY

2

British Library Cataloguing in Publication Data:
McGrail, Seán
Ancient Boats and Ships. – 2nd ed. – (Shire archaeology; 31)
1. Ships – Europe – To 1500
2. Boats and boating – Europe – History – To 1500
3. Underwater archaeology
I. Title II. McGrail, Sean. Ancient boats
623.8'21'094
ISBN-10: 0 7478 0645 4.

Published in 2006 by
SHIRE PUBLICATIONS LTD
Cromwell House, Church Street, Princes Risborough,
Buckinghamshire HP27 9AA, UK.
(Website: www.shirebooks.co.uk)

Series Editor: James Dyer.

ISBN-10: 0 7478 0645 4; ISBN-13: 978 0 7478 0645 5.

Number 31 in the Shire Archaeology series.

First published in 1983 as *Ancient Boats*. Second edition, revised, extended and illustrated
in colour, 2006.

Printed in Malta by Gutenberg Press Ltd, Gudja Road, Tarxien PLA19, Malta.

3

Contents

List of illustrations

Acknowledgements

I am grateful to Ole Crumlin-Pedersen of the Viking Ship Museum, Roskilde, and Dr Colin Martin of the University of St Andrews for reading and commenting on an earlier draft of this text. I am also grateful to Dr Lucy Blue, University of Southampton, for her advice on chapter 5, 'Places to visit', and chapter 6, 'Further reading'.

I thank the following colleagues, who arranged for me to have colour illustrations: Professor Arne-Emil Christensen, University of Oslo; Peter Clark, Canterbury Archaeological Trust; Dr John Coates, Trireme Trust; Professor Bryony Coles, University of Exeter; Ole Crumlin-Pedersen, Viking Ship Museum, Roskilde; Dr Volker Hilberg, Schloss Gottorf, Schleswig; Kate Hunter, Newport Museum; Rear Admiral John Lippiett, Mary Rose Trust; Isabelle Robert, Directrice, Tapisserie de Bayeux; Professor Dr Lars Scholl, Deutsches Schiffahrtsmuseum; Timothy Severin, Timoleague; and Dr Patrick Wallace, Director, National Museum of Ireland. My thanks also go to Mrs Barbara Johnstone for permission to publish several photographs taken by her late husband Paul.

Glossary

Altitude: the vertical angle of a heavenly body above the sea horizon (see figure 40).

Boat: a hollowed vessel that derives its buoyancy from the displacement of water by a continuous watertight outer surface.

Caulk: to insert material between two timbers and thus make the junction watertight.

Cleat: a projection to which other fittings or a line may be fastened.

Clinker-built: a form of boatbuilding in which the *strakes* partly overlap one another, upper strake outboard of lower strake (see figure 27D).

Crook: a curved piece of wood that has grown into a shape useful for boatbuilding.

Draft: the vertical distance between the waterline and the lowest point of the hull.

Floor timbers: the lowest transverse timbers, often *crooks*, set against the bottom planking.

Fore-and-aft: a direction parallel to the centreline of a vessel.

Frame-first: a form of boatbuilding in which the keel, post and (elements of the) frames are set up and fastened before planking is fashioned.

Freeboard: the height of the sides of a boat above the waterline.

Grommet: strand(s) of rope laid up in the form of a ring.

Keel: the main longitudinal strength member, joined to the stems forward and aft.

Keelson: a centreline timber on top of the *floor timbers*, adding to longitudinal strength; it may have a *mast step* incorporated.

Knot: a speed of one *nautical mile* per hour (approximately 1.15 statute miles per hour).

Leeway: the amount a vessel is driven downwind of her course by the wind.

Logboat: a boat hewn from a single log.

Mast step: fitting used to house the heel (lower end) of a mast.

Megalith: a large stone, especially one placed upright as (part of) a monument.

Moulded: dimension of a timber measured at right angles to its *sided* dimension.

Nautical mile: 1.15 statute miles or 1.853 km.

Plank-first: a form of boatbuilding in which the planking is (partly) erected and fastened together before framing is inserted (see figure 16).

Plank-keel: a keel-like timber of which the ratio of its *moulded* dimension to its *sided* dimension is less than or equal to 0.70.

Raft: a floating structure formed by binding together individual elements, each with a specific density of less than unity; its buoyancy is derived from the flotation characteristics of each element.

Reconstruction: in this context, a process in which the structure and/or form of the non-recovered elements of an excavated boat are deduced from other evidence.

Reverse-clinker: a form of boatbuilding in which the *strakes* partly overlap one another, upper strake inboard of lower strake (see figure 51A, right).

Rove: a washer like piece of metal forced over the point of a clinker nail before it is clenched (see figure 27D).

Sheerline: the curve of the upper edge of the hull.

Ship: in this context, a large, and often complex, *boat*.

Sided: dimension of a timber measured (near) parallel to the *fore-and-aft* plane of the vessel.

Stem: the timber – often a post – at the bow of a vessel to which the planking is fastened.

Strake: a combination of planks that generally stretches from one end of a boat to the other.

Traverse tables: tables that enable a navigator to calculate a vessel's position or the course to steer.

Treenail: wooden peg or dowel used to join two timbers (see figure 27E).

Washstrake: an additional *strake* fitted to increase the height of the sides (see figure 22).

1
Introduction

Man and the sea

Two-thirds of the globe is covered by seas; the remaining third has numerous lakes and rivers, which act as both barriers and highways. Until post-medieval times these lakes and rivers had imprecise boundaries and in wet seasons considerably extended their basins and channels, while coastlines have undergone short- and long-term changes as a result of erosion, deposition and variations in sea level. From earliest times man has had both to combat and to make use of these expanses of water to explore and exploit his environment, to extend his settlements and colonise other areas, and to sustain trade and travel in later times.

Almost all significant water barriers were crossed at a remarkably early date. Even at times of much lower sea levels there was deep water between western Indonesia and New Guinea, yet archaeological evidence shows that man came to Australia from south-east Asia before 40,000 BC, possibly as early as 60,000 BC, crossing 600 nautical miles of sea strewn with islands. The American continent was also peopled from Asia, across what is now the Bering Strait, from Siberia to Alaska, sometime during the period 40,000 to 12,000 BC. At times of low sea level during these millennia it would have been possible to walk from the Old to the New World; at other times a sea voyage would have been necessary. In the Mediterranean, Mesolithic man of the tenth millennium BC was able to reach the island of Melos and transport obsidian back to the Argolid coast of Greece. Around 7000 BC deep-water fish were caught in the Mediterranean and, further north, the rising sea level, which cut off Britain and Ireland from the continent of Europe by the seventh millennium BC, obliged subsequent settlers and traders to use water transport.

There are many examples of the early use of seagoing craft to populate islands: for example, the colonisation of western Melanesia in the south Pacific by c.3000 BC, and the subsequent occupation of Micronesia and Polynesia between 1500 BC and AD 1200. Even within land masses water transport facilitated man's early expansion, as in his progress throughout the Americas from Alaska to the southern tip of South America.

Thus it is clear that from very early times neither lakes and rivers nor seas were insurmountable obstacles to man's movements. Well before he had domesticated animals, mastered agricultural and pottery skills, or constructed megaliths, he was able to build and use water transport.

Rafts and boats

I have used the expression 'water transport' above to emphasise that man used rafts as well as boats. Rafts made of logs, reeds, bark bundles or floats have had widespread use on tropical and equatorial seas and on inland waters in many zones. They differ from boats in that little attempt is made to make them watertight; they float because of the buoyancy of individual elements. Boats, on the other hand, have hollow hulls that displace water and thereby gain buoyancy; they have been made from logs, bark, reed and hides, in addition to the now ubiquitous plank boat. All these materials are perishable and thus only in special circumstances do ancient rafts and boats survive. However, on occasions representations of water transport have been carved on stones or used as decorations on seals and pots, and sometimes small model boats are found. In addition, written descriptions of rafts and boats survive from some early literate civilisations. Study of modern boat types may also help; it is possible to suggest, for example, that because hide boats are in use in the sub-Arctic today similar ones may have been in use there in prehistoric times. Such a line of argument leads to the possibility that reed-bundle rafts may have been used in prehistoric and medieval Europe, for their modern use is known in Ireland, Hungary, Sardinia and Corfu.

In northern and western Europe, the area with which this book principally deals, there is direct evidence only for logboats (dugout canoes), planked boats, hide boats and log rafts in the prehistoric and medieval periods. Other forms of water transport may have been used, but evidence has not survived or has not yet been recognised.

Maritime archaeology

The main focus of this book, the study of ancient boats and rafts, is at the heart of the wider topic of maritime archaeology, which itself merges into the mainstream of the archaeological discipline. Thus working out how an excavated boat had been built, and which tools were used, leads to an investigation of its equipment (anchors, bailers, and so on), how it was propelled and steered, loaded and discharged, and what tasks it was used for (ferrying, fishing, fighting, cargo carrying, for example). We then may ask where it was normally used and, if at sea, how it was navigated. A related topic is the study of harbour facilities such as landing places (waterfronts, beacons, leading marks, and so on), cargo-handling arrangements and warehouses, boatbuilding sites, causeways, boathouses and slipways.

Maritime artefacts and structures may be found underwater (at sea or inland), in the intertidal zone or on land. It is not only the remains of buildings that may be found on land, for boats and fish weirs may be found in former watercourses, or on land that was intertidal before being enclosed, or on land that has emerged because of relative falls in sea level. In addition, in certain times and places boats have been used in funeral ceremonies and may be found in graves. Conversely, where there has been a relative rise in sea level, buildings and other structures as well as wrecks may now be found underwater. Thus 'dry' archaeologists and 'wet' archaeologists, and those who are both, are involved in the excavation of maritime artefacts and structures. The area within which they work may be called the 'maritime zone': this extends to seaward and to landward of the present-day shoreline and includes estuaries, rivers and lakes and the land adjacent to them.

Figure 1 shows that other specialists are involved in this maritime research: botanists, zoologists, geologists and climatologists investigate the environment in which ancient craft were used; oceanographers and geographers carry out sea-level studies; dendrochronologists and radiocarbon specialists may date and determine the origin of wood; naval architects and computer scientists assess a boat's performance; historians study documentary evidence for maritime activities; art historians date and interpret representations of boats; linguists deduce the meanings of place-names; conservators preserve excavated remains and curators

1. Flow diagram of archaeological research.

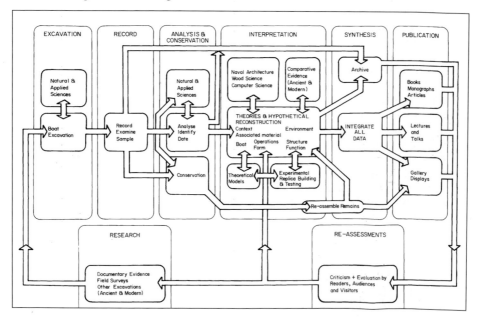

display them. Individual archaeologists may be able to undertake some of these additional tasks – historical research or naval architectural calculations, for example – but generally the post-excavation phase of a maritime project is one of teamwork, with the archaeologist as co-ordinator.

The time range of this book extends from before the European Bronze Age, and equivalent phases elsewhere, to the sixteenth century AD. Boats travel and the bigger ones may voyage widely; they may be wrecked far from their home port. They are their own advertisement and a successful design, or aspects of it, may be copied far from where it originated. In addition, a study of just one country's boat finds would reveal an incomplete and skewed picture of maritime antiquity. Thus this book deals not only with northern and western Europe but also (in less detail) with boats from other parts of the world. There have been significant finds in Mediterranean waters, especially in the east – Israel, Turkey and Greece – and from land sites in Egypt. A number of medieval vessels have been excavated in south-east Asian and Chinese waters. Elsewhere finds are sparse and the study of early, indigenous water transport is in its infancy.

How the subject developed

Logboat and plank-boat remains were found in many places in Europe from the seventeenth century onwards: logboats were declared to be 'primitive' and therefore 'prehistoric'; plank-boat remains were said to be 'Viking'. None of the finds was adequately documented and few were preserved. A late-medieval vessel found in Kent near the River Rother in 1822 is typical of this phase of archaeology. After being excavated (figure 2), lifted and put on display, the extensive remains were destroyed when the owner could no longer make a profit. In 1958 a boat from the second century AD was exposed when foundations for an extension to Guy's Hospital were being dug near the Thames, at the southern end of London Bridge. Only very limited recording could be undertaken. Although the site was scheduled in 1983 as an ancient monument, it seems likely that little of this Romano-Celtic boat now survives as the water table has fallen below the level of the remains, allowing the timber to dry out and decay – another lost opportunity.

The latest phase of maritime archaeology may be said to have begun in 1863 with Conrad Engelhardt's excavation of three boats from a bog at Nydam in southern Jutland. One of these survives and is on display in the museum at Schloss Gottorf, Schleswig (figure 3). Engelhardt recorded many details of this boat and, although there are doubts about the way the remains have been reassembled (including the addition of modern wood), the remains and the documentation have proved sufficient for

2. The 1822 excavation of a medieval vessel from a former bed of the River Rother, Kent.

late-twentieth-century Danish scholars to determine the most likely form of the original fourth-century AD boat.

In the late nineteenth and early twentieth centuries several ships were excavated from Viking age burial mounds in Norway (figure 4). This spectacular group of finds fired public interest and stimulated research into Viking age boatbuilding, which continues today. To explain these finds, Scandinavian scholars drew on medieval documentary evidence, including the Icelandic sagas, and found analogies for form and fittings in the contemporary boats of western Norway. Such was the interest in these ships that a full-scale reconstruction of one of them, the ninth-century Gokstad ship, was built and sailed from Norway to the United States in 1893.

During this early phase, commercial divers, fishermen and sponge divers occasionally brought to the surface objects from wreck sites, but the potential thus indicated could not be fully realised until the invention of the aqualung by Cousteau and Gagnan. From around 1948 divers with this equipment were able to work in relative freedom on the seabed, in and around wreck sites. Archaeologists took up diving and in 1960 George Bass set the standard for underwater research in his pioneering

3. The fourth-century AD Nydam boat on display in Schloss Gottorf, Schleswig. (Dokumentationsarchiv, Archäologisches Landesmuseum)

4. The early-ninth-century Viking ship from Oseberg during excavation in 1904. (Museum of Cultural History, University of Oslo, Norway. Photograph by O. Vaering)

excavation of the late Bronze Age wreck site off Cape Gelidonya, Turkey.

Archaeology on underwater sites has made much progress since those early days. The general public may be aware only of the recovery of spectacular artefacts – amphorae and statues in the Mediterranean, coins and guns in northern waters – but the real advance has been in the standard of surveying, recording and excavating, which is now comparable with that used on land sites. The differing attitudes to wreck sites of the archaeologist, the sports diver and the commercial exploiter have at times led to conflict, and so attempts have been made to regulate the use of the seabed by these various interests so that there is minimum loss of archaeologically valuable information. In Britain underwater wreck sites may be designated as of archaeological, historic or artistic importance, and may then be investigated only by an authorised team led by an archaeologist and having access to conservation facilities. The great majority of underwater sites so far investigated in the seas around the British Isles have been of post-medieval ships; in general, on the few earlier sites only cargo has survived, not the ship's structure. In the Baltic, however, medieval as well as post-medieval vessels have been investigated underwater, and early Phoenician, Greek and Roman wrecks

5. The Swedish royal ship *Vasa* of the early seventeenth century being manoeuvred into dock after recovery. (Swedish Maritime Museum and Warship *Vasa*)

have been excavated in the Mediterranean.

Underwater excavation and salvage work have reached such a standard that almost complete ships can be raised: the early-seventeenth-century wreck of the Swedish royal ship *Vasa* was raised in 1961 (figure 5); and the remains of the Tudor warship *Mary Rose* (figure 6) were recovered from the waters of Spithead in 1982. These are exceptional cases, however, as the costs are tremendous, not least the twenty or so years of conservation that must follow the recovery of the waterlogged hulls and their contents. When such resources are not available underwater remains must be recorded on the seabed to such a standard and in such detail that small-scale models can be built or computer drawings compiled. If practicable, important elements of the structure may be lifted so that details can be confirmed. In this way the maximum of information can be retrieved without the heavy costs of salvage, post-excavation research, and the conservation and display of a hull and contents.

The long-standing Scandinavian interest in maritime archaeology was further stimulated by the Danish excavation in 1958–62 of five Viking age boats that had been sunk in the eleventh century AD to block Roskilde Fjord at Skuldelev. The initial evaluation and survey were carried out underwater but the excavation by Olaf Olsen and Ole Crumlin-Pedersen

6. *Mary Rose* in her recovery cradle being lowered by the lifting vessel *Tog Mor* on to a barge for transport into Portsmouth harbour in October 1982. (Mary Rose Trust)

(figure 7) was undertaken inside a protective coffer dam that kept out the waters of the fjord. The reports published on these Skuldelev ships have become a model of how to undertake post-excavation research on the remains of a wooden boat – or indeed any wooden structure.

Parallel with the upsurge in underwater archaeology has been an increase in maritime archaeology on land caused by drainage schemes, as in the Dutch polders, and by the redevelopment of dockside areas, as in Dublin, London, Copenhagen and other ports. Research excavations have also been undertaken, as at the royal burial mound at Sutton Hoo, Suffolk, where the impression was revealed of an early-seventh-century AD vessel (figure 8), some 18 metres (60 feet) long, with spectacular grave goods. Similar excavations had earlier been undertaken at Ladby,

7. The 1962 Skuldelev excavation inside a coffer dam in Roskilde Fjord. (Vikingeskibsmuseet, Roskilde)

8. Photographic montage of the excavation of the early-seventh-century Sutton Hoo ship in 1939. (Miss M. Lack)

Denmark, where the 'ghost' of a tenth-century ship was similarly exposed. Less spectacular, but of great significance to maritime archaeology, was the discovery of sewn-plank boats on the northern foreshore of the River Humber at North Ferriby, East Yorkshire. In 1937 E. V. Wright and his brother found what they at first assumed was part of a Viking ship but

9. Ferriby boat 1 exposed on the foreshore of the tidal Humber estuary in 1946. (E. V. Wright)

which subsequently proved to be from the Bronze Age (figure 9). The publication of these boats revolutionised ideas about early water transport and woodworking technology, and reminded archaeologists that there was a maritime dimension to antiquity three thousand years before the Viking age.

Many land archaeologists at some time investigate aspects of the maritime past such as trade, migration, sea-level changes and waterfront structures. But there is a core to this maritime sub-discipline – the study of water transport, which requires specialised knowledge and research techniques. In addition, artefacts recovered from waterlogged sites (whether on land or underwater) have to undergo lengthy conservation; and boats and ships that have been recovered need large premises for post-excavation research and display. Specialist units have therefore been established in the United States, Scandinavia, Germany, the Netherlands, France, Ireland, Israel and Australia; others are being formed elsewhere. The Archaeological Research Centre at the National Maritime Museum, Greenwich, was formed after the chance discovery and rescue excavation in 1970 of a late-ninth-century AD boat from a tributary of the River Thames at Graveney in Kent. The Centre undertook much fieldwork, including excavations on land, underwater and in the intertidal zone, and set up a laboratory specialising in the conservation of waterlogged materials. The information gained about the period between 2000 BC and AD 1500 was made available in books and lectures, and by displays in the museum's archaeological gallery. Financial economies led to the closure of this Centre in 1986. An unforeseen, but ultimately beneficial, outcome of this closure was that Greenwich maritime expertise was dispersed to the university sector with a healthy impact on the education and training of maritime archaeologists and historians. The principal centre for postgraduate maritime archaeology in Britain is at the University of Southampton, and in Ireland at the University of Ulster in Coleraine.

2
The maritime archaeologist at work

Excavation

Boat finds are almost never complete and are often in a fragmented and degraded state. Their propulsion outfit, their steering system and their topsides are usually missing, and the surviving timbers are frequently distorted and dispersed. Exceptions are boats and ships that have been used for burials. Although broken and distorted, a great proportion of a burial vessel and its equipment can survive to be excavated, as was the case at Oseberg (figure 4). The Sutton Hoo ship burial is also noteworthy as in the thirteen centuries between burial and excavation the wood had disintegrated, leaving only impressions of planking in the soil and rows of boat nails. Meticulous excavation by the British Museum revealed this 'ghost' ship (figure 8), and much was learned about its construction.

The Brigg 'raft' (figure 10) was first exposed in 1888 during the extraction of brick clay from the banks of the River Ancholme in north Lincolnshire. It was relocated by the National Maritime Museum in 1973 and excavated the following year. Research has shown that it was not a raft but the flat bottom and part of one side of a sewn-plank boat of the

10. The 1888 excavation of the Brigg 'raft', photographed by the Reverend A. N. Claye. (A. Hunt. 'Viking raft or pontoon bridge', *Saga Book of the Viking Club*, 5 [1907–8], 355–62)

seventh or eighth century BC. A modern example of a ship find on a land site is the late-medieval vessel encountered at Newport in south-east Wales during the construction of foundations for a theatre on the western waterfront of the River Usk (figure 11). This cargo ship had evidently been abandoned while moored stern to the land, possibly for repairs.

In the Mediterranean and the Baltic, and occasionally in British waters – as with *Mary Rose*, ancient vessels are excavated underwater. Sometimes it proves possible to remove a wreck from the water (figure 5), or to remove the water from the wreck (figure 7), and then to carry out the excavation. Alternatively the vessel may be dismantled and recovered in pieces, as is generally the case on land sites.

Excavation techniques used by maritime archaeologists are standard archaeological ones modified to suit the context of the excavation, be it on land or underwater. Descriptions may be found in some of the books listed in chapter 6. This chapter concentrates on the post-excavation phase of research, illustrating the techniques used by reference to recent work in northern and western Europe.

11. Looking towards the bow of a fifteenth-century ship during the 2002 excavation from the waterfront of Newport, south Wales. (Newport Museum and Gallery)

Recording a boat find

By careful examination of the excavated timbers much may be learned about the parent trees and about the techniques used to turn them into parts of a boat's structure. The species of wood may be identified by microscopic examination of samples; even the form of individual trees may be recognised: for example, long, straight, sound planks indicate a tall forest tree with few knots in its lower length, whereas a naturally curved timber probably came from an isolated, low-branching tree. Counting growth rings can reveal the age of the timber at felling and give some indication of the rate of growth, which may throw light on early techniques of woodland management. We may also learn how planking was converted from the log – by splitting the log radially, as was generally done for oak, or by fashioning planks in the tangential plane, as for pine. The former presence of missing timbers is indicated by patterns of fastening holes or impressions left in the wood where two timbers were in contact. Tool marks may also be detected and these may be related to particular tool types. Wear marks may suggest how a boat was rigged, propelled and steered, or they may indicate stresses imposed on the hull when underway. Marks on the keel or bottom planking may indicate the use of hard beaches as landing places.

By this sort of detailed examination it is possible not only to deduce something about parts of the boat that have not survived, but also to infer the building sequence and the woodworking techniques used by the builder, and to learn about aspects of the boat's use.

As part of the investigative process, scale drawings or full-scale tracings are made of every individual timber. Important features are recorded at full scale and photographed. The traditional method of drawing by measured offsets is only one way in which a boat can be recorded; photography, photogrammetry (machine plotting of contours or details seen in three dimensions from a pair of stereo photographs) and plaster moulds (as at Sutton Hoo) have also been used, and computer-assisted methods are increasingly employed.

It is also essential to take direct measurements of important features – for example the angle of slope of lengthening joints or scarfs in the planking, the spacing between plank fastenings, and the diameter of nail holes, for even if these appear on scale drawings or photographs precision will be lost if measurements can be recovered only by scaling up.

Interpretation

Excavation and post-excavation records provide the information upon which hypotheses can be based. The first step in interpretation is to establish the original shape of the boat, and one of the best ways of investigating this is to make a small-scale (say 1:10) model of each

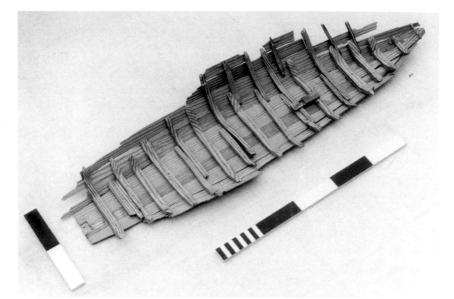

12. The 'as found' scale model of the Barland's Farm Romano-Celtic boat, based on post-excavation measured drawings of individual timbers. (Newport Museum and Gallery)

element excavated, in cardboard, balsa wood or other light timber. Fastening holes and marks made by adjacent timbers are included, and any post-depositional distortion or shrinkage is allowed for when marking out the shape of these models. The modelled parts are then assembled by bringing fastening holes into line and placing displaced timbers on their marked positions: something close to the original form and structure of the incomplete boat should then emerge (figure 12).

The next stage is to extend this 'as found' model of the boat and attempt to establish the shape and structure of its missing parts (figure 13). It is usually safe to assume that a boat was symmetrical about the fore-and-aft line (although examples of non-symmetrical boats are known), but defining the upper edge and the ends of the hull can be difficult unless parts of them have been recovered. Some progress may be made, however, by calculating the change in freeboard, draft and stability as each additional hypothetical plank or other timber is added to the reconstruction drawing or model; such calculations will indicate whether seaworthiness and cargo capacity are improved or affected adversely by this element of the reconstruction process. The positioning of fittings can also be checked: if it is thought, for example, that a rudder or an oar pivot should be in a certain position then it must be confirmed that men

13 A reconstruction scale model of the Barland's Farm boat based on the 'as found' model in figure 12. (Newport Museum and Gallery)

sitting or standing at the appropriate station could actually use them.

A study of other excavated boats from the same period and building tradition may also suggest how broken or missing parts of the find should best be theoretically reconstructed. Modern analogies may also help: study of the methods used in twentieth-century small-scale pre-industrial boatbuilding (as still survive in places such as southern India) can reveal a range of technical solutions to such general problems as how to close the ends of a boat or how to make one watertight. The excavated evidence may then be re-examined in the light of these possibilities. Such research may also suggest possible uses for timbers of an unusual nature found associated with a boat find but not fastened in position.

Ancient models or representations of boats and ships on pots, coins, town seals or paintings may similarly be a source of ideas for interpreting remains and an aid to the hypothetical reconstruction of their full form. These sources are especially useful for rigging and sails, which very rarely survive. Nevertheless, as with ancient and modern analogies, such evidence must be critically assessed: its compatibility with the excavated remains and with the ancient technological environment must be demonstrated before it can be used with confidence as an aid to reconstruction.

There may well be more than one solution to the problem of reconstructing the original form of a boat: where only the bottom is excavated, several forms of topsides may be compatible with it. If part of the sides also survives this range of possibilities is reduced; nevertheless, several reconstructions can still be compatible with the excavated remains. Such reconstruction models and drawings of variant solutions are hypotheses, not to be confused with the original. They may be close to the original form but new evidence may emerge when the boat timbers are reassembled after conservation or from future excavations of similar boats, and improved research techniques may one day show that aspects of the reconstructions are wrong: in any of these cases the drawings and models will have to be revised.

From these hypothetical reconstructions deductions may be made about the size of a boat's crew and how much cargo she could have carried. Estimates may also be made of speed, stability and seaworthiness in different sea states. Certain parameters must be fixed, however, before this can be undertaken: we must, for example, determine the sort of loads likely to have been carried, and the weight and height of crew, passengers and animals may also be significant in stability calculations. In addition, it is necessary to establish the range of drafts within which such boats would have been used. It is common practice to use a draft of 60 per cent height of sides amidships for cargo ships and 50 per cent for warships as standards for comparison between reconstructed vessels. It can be seen, therefore, that a single statement about performance can seldom be made: rather, a range of values is given, reflecting the variability in the different assumptions made, the parameters adopted and the alternative hypothetical reconstructions postulated.

Experimental archaeology

Sometimes it proves possible to test hypothetical reconstructions by building a full-scale model and undertaking trials. When pursued rigorously, these experiments take a long time and are expensive. Experimental research in archaeology requires as much planning as in any scientific discipline, and it is essential to have the evidence, the research methods and the reconstruction models and drawings examined and validated by a range of specialists before the project becomes committed to building a boat.

In 1972–3 the National Maritime Museum built a full-scale model of the smallest of the three boats found inside the Viking Gokstad ship in its burial mound. The reassembled remains of this ninth-century *faering* (four-oared boat) are housed in the Viking Ship Hall, Oslo (figure 14). The aims of this Greenwich experiment were to learn about Viking age boatbuilding and seamanship and gain experience so that authentic

14. The ninth-century Gokstad *faering* (four-oared boat) on display in Oslo. (Museum of Cultural History, University of Oslo, Norway)

15. Preparing to launch the Greenwich reconstruction of the Gokstad *faering* in Plymouth harbour.

16. Building the Roskilde reconstruction of Skuldelev 3 in 1983: after floor timbers had been fastened to the bottom planking, the side planking was fitted. (Vikingeskibs-museet, Roskilde)

experiments could be undertaken in the future. The 6.51 metre (21 foot) boat was built by Harold Kimber, a master boatbuilder from Somerset, using measured drawings of the original prepared by Arne Emil Christensen of Universitetets Oldsaksamling, Oslo, and sea trials were undertaken in the tidal reaches of the River Tamar at Plymouth (figure 15). The boat's performance was assessed as objectively as possible in different rowing and steering configurations, with varying loads, and in a range of weather conditions.

Since the 1980s the Viking Ship Museum at Roskilde, Denmark, has built full-scale models of reconstructions of each of the five medieval Skuldelev wrecks (figure 16) and undertaken trials in Roskilde Fjord

17. Inside the Vikingskibs-museet at Roskilde: Skuldelev 6 in the foreground; Skuldelev 1, 2 and 3 to the rear. (Vikingeskibs-museet, Roskilde)

and in the open seas. Preliminary reports on this unprecedented series of experiments have been enthusiastically welcomed by the academic community and the wider world; definitive reports were in preparation in 2005.

Conservation and display

If excavated boat remains have been considered of sufficient importance to warrant recovery, they will become important primary evidence and may also prove to be of great interest worldwide. It is thus essential that they are conserved by a method that maintains their excavated form and dimensions as closely as possible. Recently deposited timbers that are only slightly degraded may be stabilised by allowing them to dry slowly, but more degraded timbers, which would shrink excessively if dried, require some form of active conservation.

Several conservation methods have been used on waterlogged wood, including immersion in a tank of polyethylene glycol (PEG), a wax that is soluble in water; spraying with PEG; and freeze drying. Depending on the internal degradation of the timber, two of the treatments may be used in succession. The process, whether by spray or by immersion, is a long one, taking years rather than months.

In the Roskilde display of the Skuldelev vessels only original wood is displayed, and the deduced full shape is outlined in metal framing (figure 17). This method shows one solution to the reconstruction problem. An alternative is to display the remains (or full-scale models of them) without added reconstruction and to present several small-scale reconstruction models nearby.

Publication

The information about a boat find obtained from recording (on site and during post-excavation research), small-scale model building, experimental research and reassembly for display has to be integrated to form a coherent whole. To this is added information from the artefacts found with or near the boat. Dating evidence must be evaluated and the environmental context in which the vessel was deposited determined. The identification of pollen and of other floral and faunal remains within the boat may enable a picture to be built up of the vessel's use and suggest the types of cargo carried.

As figure 1 shows, the end of an archaeological investigation is the publication of a synthesis of all the evidence by book, lecture and display. In this way knowledge of the find is disseminated, and interpretations and deductions become subject to criticism and evaluation. In a sense, a project is never finished: publication stimulates other projects, theoretical and practical, and thus progress is continually made.

3
Water transport in north-west Europe

Early man's technological abilities as seen in his tools and artefacts suggest that during the European Upper Palaeolithic period (c.40,000 to 8000 BC) he was capable of building rafts of reed, bark or logs, and simple hide boats. By early Neolithic times (c.4000 BC) all the basic types of water transport, including plank boats, could theoretically have been built. There are, however, no finds of water transport from these periods to confirm such speculations except for some logboats, the earliest of which are dated to the early seventh millennium BC (see page 32). The earliest known plank boats in north-west Europe – those from the River Humber (see page 35) – are from c.2000 BC. Caesar described how the Celts used log rafts to cross the River Rhine, and two rafts dated to the second century AD have been excavated at Strasbourg; otherwise there is little information about rafts in northern and western Europe until the post-medieval period. The main evidence of water transport is thus for logboats from the late Stone Age onwards, plank boats from the Bronze Age onwards, and hide boats and log rafts from Roman times. Theoretically reed-bundle rafts and bark boats could also have been used in early north-west Europe, but evidence for them has not yet been recognised.

Logboat remains are the most numerous, but many of them were found before the mid twentieth century and were seldom well recorded or dated. A number of more recently excavated prehistoric and medieval plank boats are well documented, but these are unevenly spread over north-west Europe and their dates range over a period of more than three thousand years. Several of these are mere fragments and contribute little to our understanding of the past. There is, however, some clustering of finds where several boats in a region appear to be from the same building tradition and the same period: the River Humber in late prehistoric times; the River Rhine, southern Britain and Guernsey during late Roman times; before, during and after the Viking age in Scandinavia; and the region between the Rhine and the Baltic in the later Middle Ages. Only from these groups can useful generalisations be made and so, rather than a continuous history of water transport in northern and western Europe, we have a few blocks of information, valid for certain regions and limited periods of time, with only slight indications of what happened at other times and places. Documentary and iconographic evidence may add to this archaeological picture, but there are still great gaps in our knowledge.

Names of ship types are mentioned in medieval documents but not all finds can be allocated to such types. Even more rarely can the name of a find be established. Most finds from before AD 1600 are anonymous, being now identified by a site name and sequential number: Sutton Hoo 2, Ferriby 3, and so on. Exceptions to this include a fifteenth-century wreck in the River Hamble near Bursledon in Hampshire, which, from documentary and dating evidence, seems almost certainly to be Henry V's *Grace Dieu*, and the wreck of Henry VIII's *Mary Rose*, on display in the naval base at Portsmouth.

Hide boats

There is some evidence for hide boats (skin boats) during the Bronze Age but it is neither plentiful nor strong. Rock carvings in northern Scandinavia and Russia have been interpreted as representations of them but such carvings are difficult to interpret and date. A small model, made of shale, from Caergwrle, Flintshire, which is usually dated to the Bronze Age, has also been taken to represent such a boat. Not until Roman times is there significant evidence. Caesar and Pliny describe the use of hide boats in Italy, Spain and Britain, and the *Massaliote Periplus*, an early form of pilotage book, indicates that seagoing versions were used for sixth-century BC voyages between Brittany, Britain and Ireland. An 18 cm (7 inch) gold model from Broighter, near Limavady in County Derry in the north of Ireland, may represent this type of boat (figure 18). This

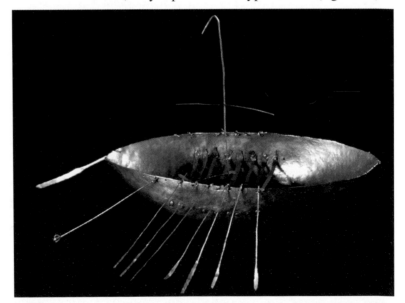

18. Gold model boat of the first century BC from Broighter, County Derry. (National Museum of Ireland)

first-century BC model, which was part of a hoard discovered in the mid nineteenth century, has nine pairs of oars, and a mast and yard show that sail was also used; steering was by an oar over the quarter. Also with the model were boat hooks, and poles probably used for punting.

Hide and the insubstantial timbers used for the framework of a currach or coracle survive much less well than the timber of a logboat or plank boat. Hide-boat remains are therefore almost unknown, but traces are thought to have been found of ones used for burials during the Roman period in north Lincolnshire and in the early Bronze Age at Dalgety, Fife, Scotland. These remains were vestigial and neither report adds to our knowledge of their construction. A timber from the tenth-century site at Ballinderry, County Westmeath, Ireland, however, seems to be a longitudinal member of a hide-boat frame.

The use of hide boats in and around Britain and Ireland is sporadically documented from the fifth century onwards, and late-medieval boatbuilders are known to have tanned cattle hides in oak bark and fastened them to a frame of open wickerwork. Other evidence comes from a boat identified as a currach carved on the eighth-century stone cross-shaft at Kilnaruane, near Bantry in County Cork, Ireland, which seems to be propelled by eight oarsmen, each with a single oar (figure 19). Using this sort of information and a knowledge of twentieth-century boatbuilding methods from the west of Ireland, Timothy Severin built an 11 metre (36 foot) hide boat (figure 20) and in 1976–7 sailed her across the Atlantic via Iceland. She proved to have considerable stability, remaining fairly dry in rough Atlantic seas. In fair weather with two square sails she could make 30 to 60 nautical miles (50–100 km) a day, but made considerable leeway (drift downwind) when attempting to

19. The boat carved on an eighth-century stone pillar at Kilnaruane, near Bantry, County Cork. (Paul Johnstone)

20. Timothy Severin's hide boat *Brendan* under sail in the Atlantic in 1976. (Nathan Benn/ Severin Archive)

tack to windward. This experiment has given us a general idea of the performance of an ancient seagoing hide boat.

Logboats

Logboats have been found in most European countries, the oldest ones being those from Pesse in the Netherlands and from Noyen-sur-Seine in France, which are both dated *c*.7000 BC. The oldest British logboat is that from Locharbriggs in Dumfries and Galloway, of *c*.2000 BC. An impressive oak logboat of *c*.300 BC was excavated at Hasholme in East Yorkshire from a low-lying field that was formerly a tidal creek of the Humber estuary (figure 21). She measured 13 metres in length, 1.40 metres maximum breadth and 1.25 metres in height at the stern (43 x 4.5 x 4 feet), and would have achieved good speeds with a full crew of eighteen paddlers and two helmsmen. Her size and some of her features suggest that she had a prestige role, although, if required, she could have carried up to 8 tonnes of cargo with a five-man crew. Many other logboats are shorter than the Hasholme boat, ranging from 3 to 5 metres (10 to 16 feet) in length, and were probably more useful than her as river ferries and for fishing, fowling and the transport of reeds and other raw materials.

The Hasholme boat demonstrates the wide range of woodworking techniques used at that time: a transom board caulked with moss and wedged into a groove at the stern; two bow elements fastened to the

21. The Hasholme logboat of *c*.300 BC during excavation in 1984 – stern nearest camera.

main hull by large treenails through cleats; wooden beam ties holding the sides of the boat together; washstrakes fastened on either side of the bow by treenails locked by wooden keys or cotters; a dovetailed repair similarly fastened to the hull; and *oculi* shapes carved into the hull on either bow as the 'eyes' of the boat (figure 22). This boat is now in Hull Maritime Museum, under conservation.

A logboat from Poole Harbour, Dorset, dated to the third or fourth century BC, has the underside of the bow fashioned into the shape of a

22. The reconstructed Hasholme logboat shown 'exploded'.

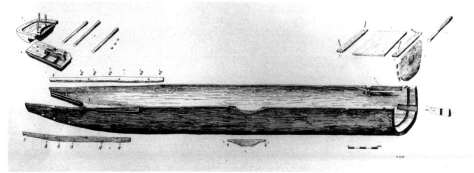

stem (figure 23), indicating that her builders were familiar with plank
boats with stems. This logboat, in the maritime museum at Poole, was
made from one half of an oak log that had been split longitudinally,
unlike the Hasholme boat, which had been hollowed from a whole log.
The 11 metre (36 foot) Poole boat was able to carry 1.72 tonnes of cargo
and four men in less than 40 cm (16 inches) of water, or eighteen men in
less than 30 cm (1 foot) of water.

Many of the European logboats so far dated are from after the first
century AD: thus not all logboats are prehistoric, as was assumed in the
nineteenth century. The latest logboat surviving in Britain is that from
Giggleswick Tarn, in western North Yorkshire, of the late fourteenth
century AD. This 2.45 metre (8 foot) logboat is unique in Britain, having
been made from an ash log rather than oak. Specially shaped timbers
had been fitted across the ends to prevent the log from splitting. Timbers
had been fastened outboard along both sides to strengthen the boat
longitudinally and possibly to increase stability when used at deep drafts.
Thus, at a time when great royal ships such as *Grace Dieu* were being
built in the harbours of southern Britain, a modest logboat was still used
to carry heavy cargo on the lake at Giggleswick in the Yorkshire highland
zone. There is documentary evidence for the use of logboats in Ireland

23. The bow of the prehistoric Poole logboat, showing her 'stem' fashioned in the log. (Poole
Museums)

and Scotland in the seventeenth and eighteenth centuries, and in Scandinavia, Germany, Austria and elsewhere in central Europe they were used into the twentieth century.

By the time the Giggleswick boat was first recorded in 1976 it had shrunk, and this is true of almost every logboat to be seen in museums today. Unless an active conservation method is used, waterlogged wood shrinks markedly as it dries out. In some cases this will cause the boat to fragment, but even when the log remains more or less a single unit it will shrink in breadth and in height of sides (the longitudinal shrinkage being insignificant). Thus many logboats were originally some 20 per cent greater in breadth and height than they appear in museums. The majority of measurable logboats from southern Britain were originally between 2.77 and 4.65 metres (9–15 feet) in length and from 73 to 99 cm (28–39 inches) in breadth; now they are roughly the same length but their breadths have shrunk to between 60 and 82 cm (24–32 inches).

It sometimes proves possible to identify a local tradition of boatbuilding, as for example in north-west England, where between 1889 and 1971 fragments of eleven oak logboats were found on a 3 mile (5 km) stretch of the River Mersey near Warrington, and two others from riverine sites some 8 miles (13 km) north-east towards Manchester. Eight of these boats have radiocarbon dates that indicate they were used during the twelfth century AD. These boats have sufficient characteristics in common to suggest that they conformed to a local tradition in logboat building: they were made from tapering oak logs some 4 metres (13 feet) in length and had rounded ends and cross-sections; transverse timbers were fastened across the ends by treenails 2.5 cm (1 inch) in diameter; and ridges were left across the bottom near the ends, probably for the paddler to push his feet against.

A 4.3 metre (14 foot) oak oared boat (figure 24) excavated from the former lake at Kentmere, Cumbria, seems to have originally been a logboat whose rotten or damaged sides were replaced by clinker-laid planking supported by four birch ribs. It had thus been converted into a logboat extended by planking, a concept that has been postulated as the prehistoric origin of the planked boat; this Kentmere find, however, is dated to c.AD 1300. Dendrochronological dating is the preferred method but few British logboats have been so dated; moreover it has not yet proved possible to dendro-date most of the British sewn-plank boats, such as those from Ferriby, as the regional master curve has not yet been extended so far back.

Plank boats in the Bronze Age

Parts of eleven Bronze Age sewn-plank boats have been excavated from England and Wales: from the Humber region (Ferriby, Brigg and

24. The thirteenth/ fourteenth-century Kentmere boat during excavation in 1955. Four strakes had been added to the original logboat hull. (Sir David Wilson)

Kilnsea); the Severn estuary region (Caldicot and Goldcliff); the Test estuary (Testwood); and from Dover. They are all of oak and range in date from *c*.1900 BC (Ferriby 3) to *c*.400 BC (Ferriby 5), and they can be divided into two groups by their date and by the nature of their plank fastenings.

Group A consists of Ferriby boats 1 (figures 9, 25 and 27A), 2 and 3, Dover (figure 26) and Caldicot 1. They are dated to the twentieth to thirteenth centuries BC, and their planking is fastened together by individual lashings of flexible yew withies through large holes. The Dover boat also has wooden wedges through cleats as bottom plank fastenings. The fragments from Kilnsea and Testwood probably belong to this group.

Group B includes Brigg 2 (figure 10), Caldicot 2 and Goldcliff. They are dated to the eleventh to ninth centuries BC, and their planking is

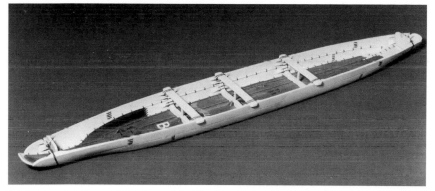

25. A reconstruction small-scale model of the Bronze Age Ferriby boat 1. (National Maritime Museum, Greenwich)

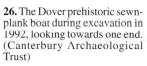

26. The Dover prehistoric sewn-plank boat during excavation in 1992, looking towards one end. (Canterbury Archaeological Trust)

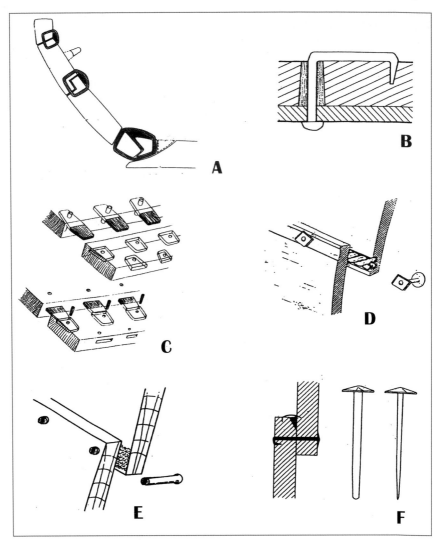

27. (A) Composite cross-section showing a Caldicot second strake fastened to a Ferriby lowest strake by yew lashings, with moss caulking held in place by a wooden lath. (B) Method of fastening the planking to the frames of the Barland's Farm Romano-Celtic boat using nails driven through a treenail and clenched by hooking. (C) Mediterranean locked mortise and tenon fastenings (after P. Pomey *La Navigation dans l'Antiquité*: 94. Édisud, Aix en Provence, 1997). (D) A Nordic plank fastening: clinker planking with hair caulking and nails clenched over a rove. (E) A Slavonic variant of the Nordic fastening: clinker planking with moss caulking and treenails. (F) Method of fastening together the Bremen cog's planking with hooked nails and moss caulking held in place by metal clamps.

fastened together by continuous stitching using two-stranded willow ropes through small holes. The fragment Ferriby 5 may also belong to this group.

Seams between the planks were made watertight by a caulking of moss held in place by a fore-and-aft lath under the stitching. The bottom planks of these boats were further linked together by transverse timbers passing through holes in cleats that projected vertically from the upper surface of the planking.

A full-scale version of Ferriby 1, based on the reconstruction shown in figure 25, would be 15.4 metres in length, 2.6 metres maximum breadth and 0.70 metres in height of sides (51 x 8.5 x 2.3 feet). Such a boat could have carried a load of 3 tonnes (crew and cargo) with a draft of only 30 cm (12 inches) and a freeboard of 36 cm (14 inches). If the freeboard were reduced to 26 cm (10 inches), which would probably be safe on a river in fair weather, 5.5 tonnes could be carried with a draft of 40 cm (16 inches).

Ferriby 1 and Brigg 2 (the so-called 'raft') are long and relatively narrow but, whereas the former is less broad towards the ends and thus has a recognisable boat form, Brigg, when reconstructed, resembles an open, rectangular box measuring some 12.30 by 2.32 metres (40 x 7.6 feet); similar boats are used on Polish rivers today. Brigg 2 was probably used as a ferry to cross the tidal River Ancholme near Brigg, where the valley narrows. With two side strakes, her overall height would have been 34 cm (13 inches), and she could have carried about 2.58 tonnes (say forty sheep and ten men), with a draft of about 25 cm (10 inches). With three strakes, her overall height would have been 55 cm (22 inches), and a load of 8.10 tonnes (say thirty cattle and ten men) would have given a draft of about 38 cm (15 inches). This Brigg boat, like other Bronze Age craft, was propelled by paddles or by poles ('punted') in the shallows.

The remains of a round-bottomed sewn-plank boat were found in the early twentieth century at Hjortspring on the island of Als, Denmark, and dated to *c*.350–300 BC. The boat was of lime wood with two strakes on each side fastened together by lime-bast cord, and the sewing holes were filled with resin. The thin planking overlapped at the edges, but with smooth outer and inner faces: this technique appears to be a forerunner of the clinker plank fastenings used in the Nordic tradition (see page 43). It is estimated that the overall length of the original Hjortspring boat was 18–19 metres (59–62 feet) with a 2 metre (6.6 foot) breadth; she was propelled by twenty paddlers. The remains are displayed in the National Museum in Copenhagen (figure 28).

Plank boats and ships in the Roman period

In his account of his first-century BC campaign against the Veneti, a Celtic people of south-west Brittany, Julius Caesar tells us that their

28. The remains of the sewn-plank Hjortspring boat in a display case at Nationalmuseet, Copenhagen. (National-museet, Copenhagen)

29. Map showing the distribution of excavated Romano-Celtic vessels: (1) Barland's Farm; (2) Blackfriars; (3) New Guy's House; (4) St Peter Port; (5) Abbeville; (6) Pommeroeul; (7) Bruges; (8) Zwammerdam; (9) Woerden; (10) Kapel Avezaath; (11) Druten; (12) Xanten; (13) Mainz; (14) Bevaix; (15) Yverden; (16) Avenches.

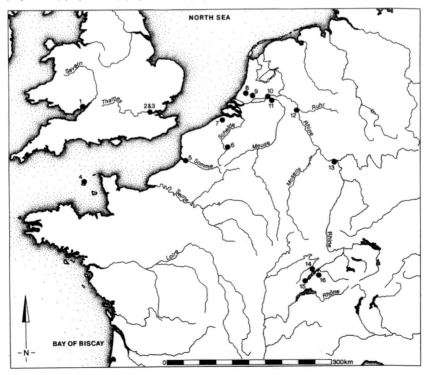

ships were different in build and in sailing rig from his own Mediterranean-style vessels. The Celtic ships were flat-bottomed with high bow and stern and had thick oak planking caulked with moss and fastened to hefty frames by iron nails 2.5 cm (1 inch) in diameter. They had leather sails and anchors with chains and were better suited to the local conditions than were the Roman vessels for, unlike the latter, they could venture inshore through shoal waters and beach safely.

During the late twentieth century a group of vessels, with common characteristics and dated to the first to fourth centuries AD, were excavated in a region stretching from the Swiss lakes, down the River Rhine to the Netherlands, to the Thames and Severn estuaries, and on to the Channel island of Guernsey (figure 29). These boats are clearly different from their contemporaries in the Mediterranean and the Baltic, and some of their features echo Caesar's description of the ships of the Veneti. It seems likely that the vessels Caesar described were forerunners of those excavated.

These vessels, now called 'Romano-Celtic', may be divided into two groups: river barges and seagoing vessels. The former have an elongated box shape (figure 30) – these were probably used on rivers and canals, where they could be towed from a towpath or, in fair winds, sailed. The seagoing sailing vessels of this tradition come from the Thames in London

30. A Zwammerdam Romano-Celtic 'barge' during excavation. (Paul Johnstone)

31. The Barland's Farm Romano-Celtic boat during excavation in 1993, looking towards the bow. (Newport Museum and Gallery)

(Blackfriars 1 ship of *c*.AD 150); the main harbour of Guernsey (St Peter Port 1 ship of *c*.AD 275); and the northern shores of the Severn estuary (Barland's Farm boat of *c*.AD 300 – figures 12, 13 and 31). A distinctive feature of these three is that they were built 'frame-first', that is, the framing was first fastened to the plank-keel and posts to define the hull shape; after that the planking was fastened to this framing by large iron nails, which were clenched by hooking the tip backwards into the inboard face of the framing (figure 27B). This building sequence is fundamentally different from that used in the contemporary Nordic and Mediterranean traditions, in which vessels were built 'plank-first': the planking was shaped and fastened together to give the hull shape; then the framing was added. The Celtic innovative, frame-first sequence was subsequently used one thousand years later to build the ships of the fifteenth- and sixteenth-century explorers such as Dias, Vasco da Gama, Columbus and Magellan. Whether there was a link between the Romano-Celtic technique and late-medieval shipbuilding in Atlantic Europe is the subject of continuing research.

Although dendrochronological work has shown that she was probably built in south-east England, a third- or fourth-century AD wreck excavated at County Hall on the south bank of the River Thames in London in 1910 had several features characteristic of Mediterranean shipbuilding, including planking fastened edge to edge by inserting tenons in mortises cut at intervals in opposing edges within the thickness of each plank. These tenons were then held in position by treenails (dowels) driven through them at right-angles (figure 27C). Other vessels found in north-west Europe with evidence for classical Mediterranean practices include two of the first-to-second-century AD Zwammerdam boats (2A and 6), excavated from the Rhine in the Netherlands, and the Vechten boat, excavated in 1893 near Utrecht. An extended logboat excavated from Lough Lene, County Westmeath, Ireland, in 1987 had oak washstrakes fastened to its logboat base in Mediterranean fashion.

Plank boats and ships in the medieval Nordic tradition

A number of boat finds from Scandinavia, the Baltic coast of Germany and Poland, Britain and Ireland, dated from the fourth century AD onwards, are of similar form, structure, propulsion and steering. The classic phase of this Nordic building tradition occurred during the Viking age (*c*.AD 800 to 1100), but ships of this general type were still being used as late as the fifteenth century – examples are Henry V's *Grace Dieu* in the River Hamble and the clinker-built ship excavated at Newport in south-east Wales (figure 11). An early member of this tradition is Nydam boat 2 of AD 310–20, on display in the Schloss Gottorf Museum, Schleswig (figure 3). She was a *c*.24 metre (79 foot) rowing boat with thin clinker planking of oak fastened together by nails clenched inboard over a metal rove (figure 27D). The central bottom member of the hull was a plank-keel (broader than deep), rather than a keel (deeper than broad), and the boat had stems at both ends, making her almost symmetrical about her midships section. The framing timbers were worked from crooks (oak branches chosen because they had the appropriate curve) and were fastened to the hull symmetrically about the plank-keel after the planking had been finished. She was propelled by fifteen oars on each side, worked in grommets against wooden pivots (tholes) projecting above the top strake of planking, and was steered by a side rudder on the starboard quarter. Sutton Hoo 2, another early boat of this Nordic tradition, survived only as an impression in the sandy soil of an early-seventh-century royal burial mound in East Anglia (figure 8).

From AD 800 to 1100 there are about thirty well-documented finds, mostly from Scandinavia, that help to construct a picture of the vessels built in the heyday of this Nordic tradition. The characteristics of pre-Viking age boats were perfected by Viking age shipbuilders. One apparent change is the introduction of the mast, for which there is excavated evidence from the eighth century; but sailing must have been prevalent in northern Europe before this time, for mast and sail can be seen on ships carved on sixth-century memorial stones from the Baltic island of

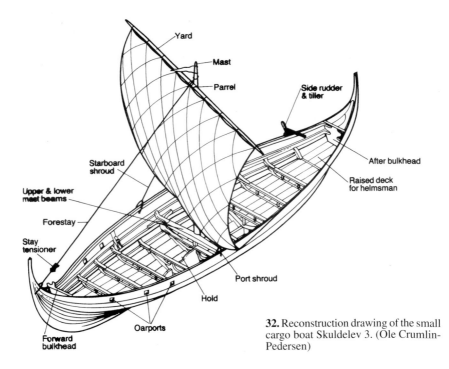

Yard

Mast

Parrel

Side rudder
& tiller

Starboard
shroud

Upper & lower
mast beams

Forestay

Stay
tensioner

After bulkhead

Raised deck
for helmsman

Port shroud

Hold

Oarports

Forward
bulkhead

32. Reconstruction drawing of the small
cargo boat Skuldelev 3. (Ole Crumlin-
Pedersen)

Gotland. The main features of Viking age shipbuilding can be seen in
figures 14, 16, 17, 27D, 32 and 33. Within this tradition, craft were built
for different functions: cargo ships, broad and deep-sided in proportion
to their length, with a hold amidships and rowing positions near bow
and stern; warships, with a full complement of rowing stations and long
in proportion to their breadth; and smaller boats, with many of the
longship's features, but used as ferries or for fishing. During this period
of three hundred years or so there were developments in building
practices, such as different methods of fastening the framing to the
planking, and variations in the number and position of crossbeams. These
and other features (such as sail and rigging, for which there is little direct
evidence) have been investigated by the research team of the Viking
Ship Museum at Roskilde, Denmark.

Ships and boats built on the southern Baltic coast, from the base of the
Jutland peninsula eastwards beyond the River Vistula/Wista, had many
of the characteristics described above but one important difference is
that the overlapping, clinker planking was fastened together by small,
headed and wedged treenails rather than iron nails, with a caulking of

moss rather than hair or wool (figure 27E). Several of the boats built in this Slavonic variant of the Nordic tradition have a mast stepped in a floor timber rather than a keelson – it is not clear whether this is also a Slavonic characteristic or whether it reflects the small size of the vessels excavated to date.

From the 1960s onwards several full-scale reconstructions of Nordic craft have been built in Scandinavia (figure 16), and in 1972–3 one was built in Britain. The National Maritime Museum at Greenwich built a *faering*, the smallest of three boats found inside the ninth-century Gokstad royal burial ship (figures 14 and 15). During trials the boat achieved an unexpectedly high speed of 7 knots under oars in Plymouth Sound. Theory indicates that such slim light-displacement craft should indeed have high speed potential: it seems likely that this is achieved in favourable conditions when the vessel rides up in the water into a semi-planing attitude. Keels, deep in relation to their breadth, and steep lower strakes suggest that Viking hulls had a respectable windward performance. How close they could get to the wind has been investigated afloat in full-scale reconstructions of the five Skuldelev ships that, since 1980, have been built at the Viking Ship Museum and sailed in Roskilde Fjord and elsewhere in the Baltic (figure 33).

33. *Havhingsten fra Glendalough*, the Roskilde reconstruction of Skuldelev 2, in Roskilde Fjord in 2005. (Vikingeskibsmuseet, Roskilde)

34. The AD 1329 town seal of Stralsund, northern
Germany, showing a cog.

The cog tradition

During the early Middle Ages the
Frisians of the Rhine estuary and
islands established themselves as
capable seafarers: they played a
prominent part in Anglo-Saxon
maritime affairs and traded with the
Baltic. A type of craft known as a
'cog', mentioned in ninth-century and
later documents, was evidently
prominent in this Frisian trade. In the
1950s Fliedner established a link between this
type name and ships depicted on Stralsund town seals of the thirteenth
and fourteenth centuries with clinker side planking and a single mast
and square sail (figure 34). Changes in the cog can be seen on these
seals: the stern rudder replaced the side rudder in *c*.AD 1245, for example,
and a false stem was introduced in *c*.1280.

A most important source of information about the late phase of cog
building is a 23.50 metre (77 foot) wreck found in 1962 during dredging

35. The Bremen cog of AD *c*.1380, having been conserved, on display in the Deutsches
Schiffahrtsmuseum at Bremerhaven. (Deutsches Schiffahrtsmuseum)

operations in the River Weser near Bremen. It had the characteristic full form and clinker sides, with angular longitudinal transitions from bottom to posts. This cog, dated by dendrochronology to *c*.1380, is on display in the maritime museum at Bremerhaven (figure 35). Diagnostic features of the late-medieval cog are: the bottom planking is laid edge-to-edge over most of its length and is not fastened together or to the plank-keel; the side planking and the bottom planking near the stems are overlapping and are fastened together by iron nails clenched inboard by turning the tip back into the timber (figure 27F) – resembling the technique used to fasten planking to framing in the Romano-Celtic tradition (figure 27B); and the caulking of moss is kept within the seams by laths and butterfly-shaped iron clamps. Most cogs so far excavated have thick, sawn planking, unlike the thin, radially split planking of the Nordic tradition. The earliest known cog – the mid-twelfth-century cog from Kollerup in Danish waters – has her mast stepped at about 29 per cent of the waterline length from her bow; the masts of later cogs are closer to midships at 34 to 43 per cent.

The *hulc* tradition

In 1956 the German scholar Heinsius established a link between early references to a ship type known as a *hulc* and a particular style of vessel in medieval depictions when he pointed out that the Latin inscription on the town seal of New Shoreham in Sussex referred to this *hulc*. In profile the Shoreham ship is double-ended, with castles at bow and stern (figure 36). There are no visible stems, and a keel is not discernible. The planking, which appears to be laid in reverse clinker, runs in a curve, parallel to both the sheerline and the bottom of the hull, and ends on a horizontal line at the base of each castle, well above the waterline. This is clearly different from both the Nordic and the cog types. Many representations of ships with similar features have been traced, including the ship on the

36. The AD 1295 seal of the Sussex town of New Shoreham, formerly known as 'Hulkesmouth'. (National Maritime Museum, Greenwich)

twelfth-century fonts in Winchester Cathedral (figure 37) and in
Zedelgem Church near Bruges. It might be thought that the depiction of
reverse clinker is an engraver's or mason's mistake, but the technique is
certainly practicable, being used in modern boatbuilding in Bangladesh,
West Bengal and Orissa (figure 51A, right), and the medieval craftsmen
should be given the benefit of the doubt.

Late medieval developments

By the end of the fifteenth century three-masted ships had become
almost commonplace in Atlantic Europe. But increase in sail power was
not the only change: most large ships were now being built 'frame-first',
that is, unlike the great majority of their predecessors, a skeleton of
timbers was first built to a predetermined shape (the ship was 'designed')
and the hull planking was fastened to it, probably in a stepwise sequence
– first some of the lower framing, then some planking, and so on. Earlier
vessels (those of the Nordic and cog traditions, but not Romano-Celtic)
had been built 'plank-first', the shell of planking being first built 'by
eye' or with the aid of simple devices, and the supporting framing being
then fastened to it.

Frame-first building techniques created stronger ships that could absorb
the stresses of several masts and sails and accept gunports through their
sides; they could carry relatively more cargo and sail further without
replenishment. These were the ships in which Europeans 'discovered'
all the seas of the world within the space of fifty years during the late
fifteenth and early sixteenth century. This shift in shipbuilding techniques

37. The twelfth-century font in
Winchester Cathedral with a
scene from the life of St
Nicholas. (The Dean and
Chapter, Winchester Cathedral)

appears to have originated in Iberian waters during the early fifteenth century. The early days of Portuguese and French frame-first shipbuilding are a continuing subject of research, as is the search for evidence for the use of this building technique in the years after the apparent demise of the Romano-Celtic frame-first tradition in the fourth century AD (see page 41).

Propulsion and steering

Wooden, paddle-shaped objects have been excavated from European Mesolithic sites: similar ones may have been used to propel rafts and boats from very early times. Model oars worked through grommets were found with the first-century BC model boat from Broighter (figure 18), and 'punt' pole terminals are known from Roman times: earlier use is likely. Sail was in use in the Mediterranean from at least 2000 BC (figure 48), but the earliest evidence for indigenous sail in north-west Europe is the mast and yard on the Broighter model and Caesar's description of the sails of the Veneti (see page 39). In Scandinavia and the Baltic documentary and iconographic evidence suggests that the sail was used there from at least the sixth century AD.

Most representations show a rectangular sail that is broader than it is deep, although an early Celtic sail appears to have been deeper than broad and fitted with horizontal battens and a boom. Until the fifteenth century the single square sail on a yard and a mast stepped near amidships seem to have been the general rule in northern and western Europe.

Vessels can be steered by the same paddle, pole or oar used for propulsion, but an independent means of steering is usually needed with a sail. The earliest form seems to have been a specially shaped paddle; steering oars were used over the stern in the early centuries AD and probably much earlier. The side rudder emerged in the pre-Viking age, while the twelfth-century *hulc* depicted on the Winchester font seems to have the earliest European representation of a median rudder (figure 37).

4
Rafts, boats and ships worldwide

Early overseas voyages

There were seamen before there were farmers, and boatbuilders before there were wainwrights. When water transport was first used on lakes and rivers will never be known but it must have been before 40,000–60,000 BC, when the island continent of Greater Australia was peopled from south-east Asia (figure 38). These were times of low sea level; nevertheless, water transport was needed to travel through the archipelago of islands that lay between the extended mainland of south-east Asia and Greater Australia. These migration voyages, from island to island for an overall distance of some 600 nautical miles (1100 km), were probably undertaken over a period of several generations.

Use of water transport may thus be as old as mankind. Indeed, research on the Indonesian island of Flores suggests that archaic hominids were established there *c*.750,000 BC: their migratory voyage from mainland south-east Asia would have involved crossing deep-water channels up to 18 nautical miles (33 km) in breadth.

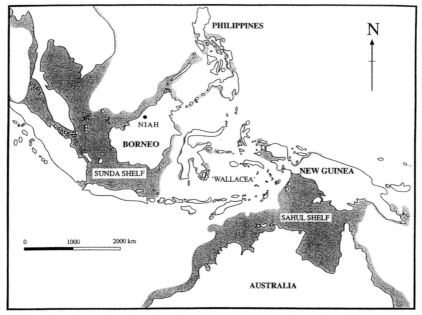

38. Map of south-east Asia (*Sunda*) and Greater Australia (*Sahul*) at a time of lower sea level. The shaded regions, now sea, represent areas that were land in *c*.40,000 BC.

These voyages in Indonesian waters are the earliest so far known, and there may well have been comparable early overseas passages elsewhere. Similarities between early stone tools of southern Spain and France and those of north-west Africa have generated the suggestion that the Strait of Gibraltar may have been crossed around one million years ago. At that time of lower sea levels this strait was 4 to 6 nautical miles (7–11 km) wide with islands usable as intermediate landing places. This remains a hypothesis; the earliest reliable evidence for a Mediterranean overseas voyage comes from the western Aegean in the tenth millennium BC: tools of obsidian quarried on the island of Melos have been excavated from the Franchthi cave on the Greek mainland. The direct route on such a voyage would have been a passage of 50 nautical miles (92 km), but an indirect route through the western Cycladic islands seems more likely, with distances of less than 15 nautical miles (28 km) between islands.

Pilotage and navigation

We may conclude that such early voyages of exploration and settlement were undertaken during daylight, in fair weather and good visibility, when land was always in sight, either astern or ahead. On such voyages pilotage techniques were used: seamen became familiar with landmarks and seamarks that indicated their whereabouts. The only instruments they might have had would have been the sounding pole or lead and line, both seen on Egyptian model boats of the third millennium BC. Lead and line could be used not only to measure the depth of water and thus help the mariner avoid running aground, but also to obtain an indication of position from the nature of the sample of the seabed recovered.

Many Mediterranean islands were settled during Neolithic times, and some of these, for example Malta, Cyprus and the Balearics, could not have been reached by paddled or oared craft during daylight hours other than at midsummer. Such restrictions may have led to the use of navigational, rather than pilotage, techniques when land was no longer visible. At the very least these seamen (and others at a similar technological stage, elsewhere) would probably have been able to get their directions from the Pole Star or, with less accuracy, from the wind or the swell.

By the mid second millennium BC, when the south Pacific began to be settled from western Melanesia and south-east Asia, voyages of several days' duration between widely spaced islands meant that, for much of this time, land was not in sight. From at least this time, therefore, advanced methods of non-instrumental navigation must have been in use (see page 64). We may conjecture that these prehistoric navigators used techniques similar to the dead-reckoning methods used by late-medieval Arabs, nineteenth-century Micronesians and early-twentieth-century North Sea trawler skippers. The aim of this non-instrumental navigation was to 'plot' on a mental chart the best estimate of the course steered and the distance run, thus defining the vessel's position relative to her home port, to a known island or point of land, or to the intended destination, all of which were out of sight.

Courses can be steered relative to a steady swell or wind, or at night by reference to the Pole Star and its circumpolar constellation (figure 39). Such guidance can be checked by noting the bearing of the sun at sunrise, sunset and noon when the sun is at its highest. A boat's speed could be assessed on a particular voyage by comparison with past performances and in the light of existing wind and sea conditions. It may also be estimated by counting the number of oar strokes used to propel the boat past a floating object thrown overboard from the bow. The earliest seagoing timepiece, the sand or running glass, did not appear until the fourteenth century AD, so earlier estimates were probably timed by chanting a standard phrase, and the speed expressed as 'faster' or 'slower than usual'. Accuracy of navigation would depend on inherited

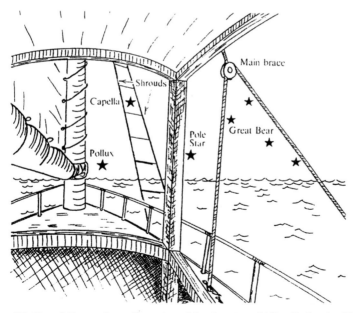

39. How Micronesian sailors steered by the stars. (After D. Lewis. *We the Navigators.* University of Hawaii Press, Honolulu, 1994. 14.)

tradition and experience, on an eye for the weather, and possibly on skills we no longer realise we possess.

Approaching land may be heralded by cloud sitting over it, by the flight line of seabirds or by the boom of the surf, and soundings by lead and line reveal decreasing depths of water. The outline shape of coastlines, especially those with high peaks or distinctive cliffs, would have been memorised, and, in later times, landmarks, beacons and church towers were built as visual aids to seafarers. Using these, the navigator would be able to identify his landfall and turn along the coast towards his destination, using favourable tidal flows whenever possible.

These non-instrumental techniques continued in use throughout the world until medieval times, when instruments began to be used: the mariner's compass in Chinese waters from the eleventh century, then in European waters from the twelfth century; sea astrolabes and other latitude-determining instruments from the fourteenth century, possibly influenced by the earlier Arab use of the star-altitude-measuring *kamal* (figure 40), itself based on the Greek angle-measuring device known as the *dioptra*. By the fourteenth and fifteenth centuries European seagoing ships had *rutters* (pilotage books), traverse tables and charts. The problem of determining longitude at sea, however, was not solved until the eighteenth century.

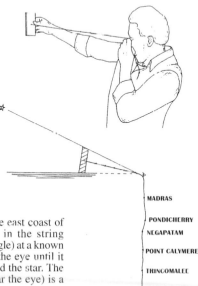

MADRAS

PONDICHERRY

NEGAPATAM

POINT CALYMERE

TRINCOMALEE

40. Method of using a *kamal*, calibrated for the east coast of India, to measure star altitudes. Each knot in the string corresponds to a given star's altitude (vertical angle) at a known port. The wooden tablet is moved away from the eye until it apparently fills the gap between the horizon and the star. The length of the string (as indicated by a knot near the eye) is a measure of the star's angle above the horizon.

Landing places

Formal landing places with wharves and jetties were not needed in north-west Europe until the tenth or eleventh century AD, except during the centuries of Roman domination. Before and after this Roman interlude craft were used from the beach within natural harbours, or from the river-bank. Alternatively, they were anchored offshore or made fast to a mooring post or stone, and men and horses waded to and from them: we see such scenes on the Bayeux Tapestry (figure 41). In tidal waters boats would take the ground on a falling (ebb) tide and be refloated either by manpower or by the rising (flood) tide. On soft, muddy sites hards of horizontal hurdles, or of poles, withies and stakes, were constructed so that boats did not stick to the mud. Such sites might also have a causeway of similar construction leading across the muddy foreshore to and from dry land.

Such informal landing places, with minimum enhancement, were used throughout the world until formal harbours began to be built, as happened in the eastern Mediterranean from the ninth or eighth century BC in an attempt to protect open sites from onshore winds and seas, to provide deeper water for bigger vessels and to alleviate the effects of silt. Similar harbours were subsequently built elsewhere as and when politics, economics and the environment determined. Nevertheless, throughout the world, away from harbours involved in overseas trade, informal landing places continue to be used by trading craft and fishing rafts and boats.

41. King Harold (carrying a hawk) and companions wading out to a ship in Bosham harbour. (Detail from the eleventh-century Bayeux Tapestry, by special permission of the City of Bayeux)

In the tenth or eleventh century AD, as north-west European towns grew and economic life became relatively complex, demand increased for low-density, mass-consumption goods, and, as a result, seagoing ships were developed in size. These larger ships could best be loaded and discharged at deep-water berths alongside wharfs; the collection of custom dues, warehouse methods of marketing and requirements to stabilise a beach or a river-bank or to enclose sea areas to gain ground reinforced this trend towards the building of formal harbours at focal points in international trading networks.

Water transport of the world

The great majority of documented early boats have been excavated from just three regions of the world: north-west Europe, the eastern Mediterranean, and Egypt. In addition a handful of boats come from south-east Asia, and a dozen medieval ships from south-east Asian and Chinese waters. In the Americas pre-Columbian logboats have been found, and there is fragmentary evidence for early hide boats in the sub-Arctic north. South Asia, Oceania and Arabia each have only one or two finds of consequence, while Australia so far has none. On the other hand, in several of these regions a range of modern traditional craft has been documented, in general terms if not yet in detail. This ethnographic recording provides a baseline from which, in favourable circumstances, documentary research can trace types of water transport back to earlier times. Ethnographic recording is urgently needed since plastic rafts and boats driven by the internal combustion engine are increasingly replacing hand-built, traditional craft propelled by muscle power, tidal flows or the wind.

A range of the basic types of raft and boat seems to be, or has recently been, used in each of the world's regions: that is, rafts of logs or of bundles (rafts of floats or pots have a more limited distribution); and boats of logs, bark (not in Europe), hide, or planks – sewn-plank boats being especially well represented. The principal exceptions to this generalisation are: bundle boats made watertight with hot bitumen have been used only in the Tigris and Euphrates area (figure 42); basket boats made watertight by a resin-based caulking only in Vietnam and Java (figure 43); and pottery boats only in India, China, Korea and Egypt. Australia seems to have had a restricted array when European explorers arrived: log rafts, bark-bundle rafts and bark boats, and extended logboats that appear to have been introduced from Indonesia into northern Australia during the fifteenth to seventeenth centuries AD.

Egypt

Rafts and boats were used by the ancient Egyptians not only on the River Nile, the country's backbone and lifeline, but also for overseas

42. A twentieth-century *zaima* reed-bundle boat of the southern Iraq marshes. (W. Thesiger. *The Marsh Arabs*. Penguin, 1978. Plate 45)

43. An early-nineteenth-century Vietnamese composite basket boat. (F. E. Paris. *Essai sur la construction navale des peuples extra-européens*. Bertrand, Paris, 1843. Plate 45)

44. Vase from Naqada, Egypt, of *c*.3100 BC, showing a craft with a single square sail. (The British Museum)

trade in the Aegean, the Levant and the Red Sea. The earliest known plank boats, the earliest depictions of sail (figure 44), sounding poles and lead and line, and the earliest known lighthouse (on the island of Pharos, at the entrance to Alexandria harbour) are all from Egypt.

In the First and Second Dynasties (3050–2686 BC), the Fourth and Fifth Dynasties (2613–2345 BC) and the Twelfth Dynasty (1991–1782 BC) boats were ceremonially buried in underground chambers within the funeral enclosures of Pharaohs or their wives. Twelve Second Dynasty boats and one Fourth Dynasty boat remain to be excavated. Of those recovered after excavation, the most striking example is the great oared vessel from an underground chamber near the pyramid of Cheops/Khufu, dated to *c*.2600 BC and on display at the Giza site (figure 45). This royal barge

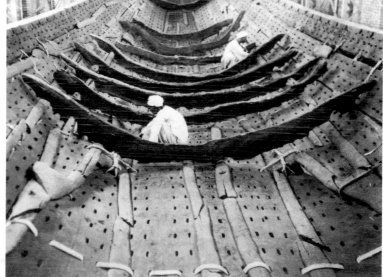

45. The interior of the Cheops ship during reassembly, with temporary fastenings in place. (Paul Johnstone)

measures 43.4 x 5.9 x 1.6 metres (142 x 19 x 5 feet) and her ends rise to 6 to 7.5 metres (20–25 feet). Her cedar planking was fastened together by unlocked mortise and tenon joints and by halfa-grass ropes running transversely across the boat's hull from topmost plank on one side to topmost plank on the other. Sixteen heavy framing timbers were then lashed to this planking. The Shire Egyptology book *Egyptian Boats and Ships* by Steve Vinson contains further details of this vessel and of many of the models and paintings of water transport excavated from Egyptian burial sites.

The *Periplus of the Erythraean Sea*, compiled in Roman Egypt during the first century AD, was a handbook for those who traded with east Africa, southern Arabia and the west coast of India; it also included pilotage information about the many harbours along these routes. Although not the earliest known *periplus*, it is one of the few dealing with the Indian Ocean.

Arabia

Excavated prehistoric finds of solidified bitumen fragments, with impressions of ropes, reeds and (rarely) planking, are probably the remains of the waterproofing outer layers of bundle boats and sewn-plank boats; this is the earliest evidence anywhere for these two boat types. The earliest fragments, from Kuwait in the Persian Gulf, are dated to the sixth millennium BC; other finds come from the upper Euphrates valley (3800 BC) and from Oman (2500–2200 BC). Apart from these

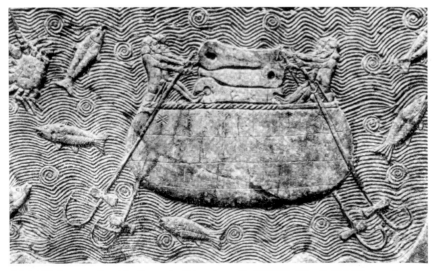

46. A hide boat depicted in Sennacherib's palace of *c*.700 BC. (The British Museum)

47. Timothy Severin's Arabian sewn-plank boat, *Sohar*, in the Indian Ocean. (Richard Greenhill/ Severin Archive)

important remains there is little surviving evidence for early water transport in Arabia. There are, however, clay models from Eridu in southern Mesopotamia, which may represent hide or bundle boats of the early fifth millennium BC, and there are other representations of water transport ranging in date from *c*.3200 BC to the early seventh century BC (figure 46). The earliest written evidence for sewn-plank boats in this region is in the first-century AD *Periplus of the Erythraean Sea*: *madarate* were built in the vicinity of Omana (to the east of the Persian Gulf) and exported to western Arabia.

A sewn-plank boat is depicted in a Mesopotamian manuscript dated *c*.AD 1237 and known as al-Hariri's Maqamat. Similar boats were noted by several medieval European travellers to Indian Ocean countries and they are still used on this coast, some rigged with an 'Arab' settee sail (a quadrilateral version of the triangular lateen sail), which has been much used on Arab vessels in recent centuries (figure 47).

Pre-Islamic Persians undertook overseas voyages, and their navigational methods were subsequently used by Arabs, who, by the tenth century AD, sailed the Mediterranean and the Indian Ocean from east Africa to Sri Lanka, and even on to China. Arab navigational techniques were described by a famed pilot, Majid al-Najdi, in the fifteenth century, and by his time lists of star altitudes (a form of latitude) had been compiled for the many places to which Arab ships sailed. The altitude (angle above the sea horizon) of Polaris and other stars was first measured in hand breadths, but from the ninth century a *kamal* was used (figure 40).

48. A sailing ship on a Minoan seal of *c*.2000 BC. (Ashmolean Museum, Oxford)

The Mediterranean

As elsewhere, surviving Mediterranean models and representations of boats are earlier than excavated examples of water transport. The former include a log raft on a fourth-century AD coin, a raft buoyed by pots on a sixth-century BC Etruscan gem, and ships with masts and rigging depicted on Minoan stone seals of *c*.2000 BC (figure 48) – the earliest evidence for sail in the Mediterranean. Early planked vessels were excavated off the south-west Turkish coast by George Bass – one off Cape Gelidonya in 1960, radiocarbon dated to *c*.1200 BC, and another off Uluburun between 1984 and 1994, dendro-dated to 'a few years after 1305 BC'. The cedar planking of these two ships was fastened together by mortise and tenon joints within the plank thickness, with the tenons locked in position by treenails (figure 27C). This joint was generally similar to that used in Egyptian ships but was locked, a technique that may have been introduced by the Canaanites/Phoenicians since the Romans knew this type of joint as *coagmenta punicana* – 'the Phoenician joint' – and its earliest known use is in a table from a mid-second-millennium BC tomb at Jericho. It has been found in excavated Mediterranean ships dated before the seventh century AD and was used when a full-scale reconstruction of a fifth-century BC Greek trireme was built experimentally in the late twentieth century (figure 49).

49. The Hellenic Navy's reconstructed trireme, *Olympias*, under 170 oars. (The Trireme Trust)

Passages in Homer, Virgil and Pliny suggest that early Greek ships had sewn planking, and a number of Mediterranean wrecks dated between 600 and 100 BC have been found to be fully sewn, or partly sewn and partly fastened by mortise and tenon joints. Subsequently the sewn-plank technique seems to have become isolated within the Adriatic, where wrecks from the late centuries BC to the eleventh century AD have been found with this feature.

Three seventh-century ships have proved to be built, at least partly, frame-first rather than plank-first, as had been universal in the eastern Mediterranean until that time. By the mid eleventh century AD, and probably earlier, fastening planks together in the plank-first sequence and building 'by eye' had been largely abandoned: a skeleton of framing was first erected to form the hull shape and then individual planks were fastened to it. Whether or not this change was influenced by the north-west European second-century AD shift to framing-first techniques in the building of Romano-Celtic vessels (see page 41) is the subject of continuing research, as is the question of how such frameworks were designed

India

Two early vessels have been found in south Asia – a sixth-century BC logboat in Sri Lanka and a flat-bottomed, possibly medieval boat with

50. *Vattai* fishing boats at a beach landing place at Eripurakarai, Tamil Nadu.

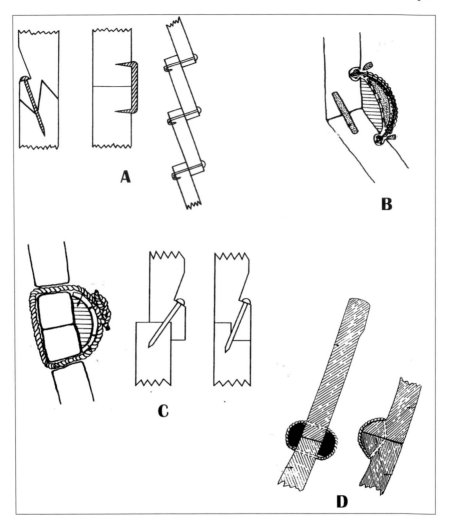

51. (A) Three twentieth-century south Asian plank fastenings: (left) angled nails (*vadhera*) in Gujarat; (centre) clamp nails (staples) in Bangladesh; (right) reverse-clinker (outboard is to the left) with hooked nails in Orissa and West Bengal. (B) Cross-section of a nineteenth-century Vietnamese boat's planking fastened by wooden dowels and locked rattan lashings (after P.-Y. Manguin. 'Sewn-plank craft of S.E.Asia', in S. McGrail and E. Kentley (editors), *Sewn Plank Boats*: figure 20.6A. BAR S276, 1985). (C) Three Chinese fastenings: (left) coir-lashed fastenings of a Hainan island boat (Manguin, 1985: figure 20.6E); and two plank fastenings with angled nails in Quanzhou ship 1 of AD 1277. (D) Maori (left) and Fijian methods of using coconut-fibre cord over a caulking to fasten planking to a logboat hull (E. Best. *Maori Canoes*: 84. Wellington Museum, 1925).

unusual structural features that in 2005 was being excavated in Kerala. In many parts of India, Sri Lanka, Bangladesh and Pakistan traditional rafts and boats are still built by hand and propelled by pole, paddle, oar and sail (figure 50). Study of these craft and of sixteenth- to nineteenth-century reports by merchants, travellers, seafarers and, latterly, ethnographers suggests how wide the range of water transport was in earlier times.

Fastenings used on modern planked boats include sewing, metal spikes, clamp nails and treenails in edge-to-edge planking, and reverse-clinker fastenings in overlapping planking (figure 51A, right). The majority of these boats were, and are, built plank-first, but *vattai* fishing boats (figure 50), and related types in Tamil Nadu, are built frame-first, using an inscribed wooden tablet to form the shape of the main frames – a technique probably derived from sixteenth-century Portuguese methods. Study of these twentieth-century Indian techniques has helped our understanding of aspects of medieval European boatbuilding.

South-east Asia

This great archipelago of islands has seen the genesis of three major overseas colonisations: that of Greater Australia in 60,000 to 40,000 BC; of the south Pacific islands in 1500 BC to AD 1200; and westwards to Madagascar in the early centuries AD. Yet the earliest excavated boats are logboats and sewn-plank boats of the second to sixth centuries AD. It seems likely that similar vessels were used much earlier, as also probably were basket boats – still widely used, some of them under sail, in Vietnam (figure 43) and eastern Java.

From the seventh to the fourteenth century boats had sewn and treenail-fastened planking (figure 51B) with frames lashed to cleats on that planking: this technique persisted, in some areas until today. From the fourteenth century large cargo ships were built with two or three layers of treenail-fastened planking, which was fastened by nails to bulkheads and to associated framing. Early accounts, by Chinese travellers as well as by Europeans, tell us that the canted rectangular sail predominated in these waters, and that steering was by twin side rudders.

China

Numerous logboats have been found inland in China, and since the 1970s several seventh- to fourteenth-century ships have been excavated in coastal waters. These medieval wrecks have constructional features similar to those of ships excavated in south-east Asian waters and may, like the south east Asian ships, have been built frame-first. There appears to have been an exchange of ideas between medieval Chinese and south-east Asian shipbuilders; which way they flowed is as yet impossible to say. The principal structural difference between the two groups is that Chinese planking was fastened together by angled metal nails (figure 51C, centre and right) rather than treenails. Other differences are that Chinese vessels used the median rudder from at least the first century AD (figure 52) rather than twin side rudders, and the battened lugsail rather than the canted rectangular sail.

Oceania

The many islands of eastern Melanesia, Micronesia and Polynesia were first settled during the centuries between 1500 BC and AD 1200, many of them on long voyages during which land was out of sight: thus advanced non-instrumental navigation had to be used (figure 39). In the late eighteenth century Captain James Cook succinctly described the methods used by these Oceanic navigators: 'the sun is their guide by day and the stars by night, when these are obscured they have recourse to the points from whence the wind and the waves of the sea come upon the vessel.' Subsequent European explorers gave more details, and in the mid twentieth century David Lewis and others studied and then practised non-instrumental methods used by Micronesian navigators. These techniques were similar to those used for millennia in the Indian Ocean, the Mediterranean and the eastern Atlantic (see page 52). An advantage that navigators in the south Pacific had was that, as their voyaging was mostly within twenty degrees of the Equator, the sun and stars rose and set much closer to the vertical than elsewhere and thus could be used longer as directional aids.

52. A Chinese pottery boat model of the first century AD. The centreline rudder is to the right; an anchor is over the bow to the left. (Guangzhou Museum)

53. A double-hull ('paired') Oceanic boat under sail, seen off Tonga in 1616. (A. C. Haddon and J. Hornell. *Canoes of Oceania: Volume 1.* B. P. Bishop Museum, Honolulu, 1936. Figure 189)

Only one excavation in this region has revealed water transport – fragments of an outrigger-fitted boat with a mast and a steering paddle from one of the Society group of islands, dated to the eighth or ninth century AD. On the other hand, European explorers from the sixteenth century onwards compiled descriptions of Oceanic craft and their unusual sailing rig, and examples and models were brought back to European museums. Four types of ocean-going sailing vessel were noted: log rafts, planked boats with and without outrigger, and plank boats with paired hulls (figure 53). It may be concluded on the basis of this late evidence that, in earlier times, outrigger boats would have been preferred for exploratory voyages and paired boats for colonisation. It also seems likely that early boats had sewn planking on a logboat base (figure 51 D) with framing lashed to cleats on the planking, and it is possible that they had a boomed triangular sail, apex down (figure 53).

The Americas

The American continent, stretching from 60°N to 50°S, was first populated along a sub-Arctic route from eastern Siberia to western Alaska, and dates suggested for this migration range from 40,000 to 12,000 BC. During periods of low sea level within that range it would have been possible to walk across what is now the Bering Strait; otherwise water transport must have been used.

From the fifteenth century AD European explorers noted a wide range of American water transport, some with unique features. Plank boats – with sewn planking – were used in only two small areas: on the Chilean coast near the Chonos archipelago, and in the waters of the Santa Barbara channel on the coast of southern California. Coastal trade was undertaken in sailing log rafts (figure 54) or sailing logboats, certain species of tree being of such great dimensions that broad, seagoing logboats could be built without recourse to stability-enhancing techniques. A special type of hide boat (*kayak*) was used off the Alaskan coasts and off the neighbouring Siberian coast (*biadarka*). A unique variant of the buoyed raft that had only two large, multi-hide floats was used at sea off the central American coast. Sail was found in use on rivers and at sea, as were double-bladed paddles, and seagoing log rafts were steered, and sail balance achieved, by the use of *guares* (figure 54), wooden foils that were thrust downwards between the logs at a number of stations to variable depths. *Guares* are similarly used in modern times on log rafts in tropical waters off south Asia, south-east Asia and southern China.

54. A seventeenth-century log raft under sail off the west coast of South America. Three of the crew are adjusting *guares* steering foils. (T. de Bry. *Grands Voyages*. 1619. Part 11, plate 12)

Future research

Since the mid twentieth century archaeologists and historians have learnt much about classical and Byzantine vessels of the Mediterranean, and about boats and ships of the Romano-Celtic and Nordic traditions of north-west Europe. Egyptian vessels of certain periods are well documented, and we are now able to list the characteristic features of a group of medieval ships from the south-east Asian and China seas. In other times and places progress is much slower, and in the particular case of prehistoric craft everywhere research is at a very early stage indeed. The earliest known logboats (European) are dated to *c.*7000 BC, the earliest known reed-bundle boats (Arabian) to the sixth millennium BC, and the earliest plank boats (Egyptian) to *c.*3000 BC. No water transport (seagoing or not) so far excavated anywhere in the world has been sufficiently early in date to have been used on those overseas voyages that we know, from other evidence, to have been undertaken before 7000 BC. There is much work to be done.

5
Places to visit

Britain

Dover Museum, Market Square, Dover CT16 1PB. Telephone: 01304 201066. Website: www.dovermuseum.co.uk Dover Bronze Age boat and prehistoric artefacts.

Hull Maritime Museum, Queen Victoria Square, Hull HU1 3DX. Telephone: 01482 613902. Website: www.hullcc.gov.uk/museums Bronze Age Ferriby boats and the Iron Age Hasholme logboat.

Mary Rose Museum, College Road, HM Naval Base, Portsmouth PO1 3LX. Telephone: 023 9275 0521. Website: www.maryrose.org *Mary Rose* ship and Tudor artefacts.

National Maritime Museum, Greenwich, London SE10 9NF. Telephone: 020 8858 4422. Website: www.nmm.ac.uk Prehistoric and medieval boats and models.

Newport Museum, John Frost Square, Newport NP20 1PA. Telephone: 01633 656656. Website: www.newport.gov.uk Caldicot and Goldcliff Bronze Age boat timbers, Barland's Farm Romano-Celtic boat and the Newport medieval ship.

Sutton Hoo Exhibition, Tranmer House, Sutton Hoo, Woodbridge, Suffolk IP12 3DJ. Telephone: 01394 389714. Website: www.nationaltrust.org.uk Early medieval burial mounds and artefacts, and a reconstruction of the central parts of the ship, including the burial chamber.

Cyprus

Kyrenia Castle, North Cyprus. Fourth-century BC Kyrenia ship.

Denmark

Ladby Ship Exhibition, Kertemunde, DK-5300. Viking ship burial site.

Nationalmuseet, Frederiksholms Kanal 12, DK-1220, Copenhagen. Website: www.nationalmuseet.dk Iron Age Hjortspring boat and artefacts.

Vikingeskibsmuseet, Vindeboder 12, DK-4000, Roskilde. Website: www.vikingeskibsmuseet.dk Five Skuldelev ships and their late-twentieth/early-twenty-first-century reconstructions, and associated artefacts.

Egypt

Egyptian National Museum, Midan el-Tahrir, Kasr el-Nil, Cairo 11557. Website: www.egyptianmuseum.gov.eg Early boats, models and artefacts.

Solar Barque Museum, Giza. Cheops ship.

Germany
Archäologisches Landesmuseum, Schloss Gottorf, Schleswig, D-24837. Website: www.schloss-gottorf.de Fourth-century AD Nydam boat and artefacts.
Deutsches Schiffahrtsmuseum, Hans-Scharoun-Platz 1, D-27568, Bremerhaven. Website: www.dsm.de Bremen cog and artefacts.
Wikinger Museum Haitabu, Schloss Gottorf, Schleswig, D-24837. Website: www.schloss-gottorf.de Hedeby ships and artefacts.

Guernsey
Guernsey Museum and Art Gallery, Candie Gardens, St Peter Port, Guernsey GY1 1UG. Telephone: 01481 726518. Website: www.museum.guernsey.net Romano-Celtic boat and medieval ship timbers and artefacts.

Ireland
National Museum of Ireland, Kildare Street, Dublin 2. Telephone: (+353) 1 677 7444. Website: www.museum.ie Broighter boat model and medieval ship timbers.

Israel
Hecht Museum, University of Haifa, Haifa 31905. Website: http://research.haifa.ac.il/~hecht Fifth-century BC Ma'agan Mikhael ship and the Athlit ship's ram.

Norway
Vikingskipshuset, Huk Aveny 35, N-0287, Oslo. Website: www.khm.uio.no/info/vskip_huset Oseberg,Tune and Gokstad Viking ships, boats and artefacts.

Sweden
Statens Maritima Museer, 10252 Stockholm. Website: www.maritima.se *Vasa* ship of 1628 and artefacts.

Turkey
The Bodrum Museum of Underwater Archaeology, Bodrum Castle, Bodrum, Mugla. Website: www.bodrum-museum.com Prehistoric and medieval ship remains.

6
Further reading

Articles on maritime archaeology and history are published in three journals: *International Journal of Nautical Archaeology*, obtainable from the Nautical Archaeology Society (Fort Cumberland, Portsmouth PO4 9LD), *Mariner's Mirror*, obtainable from the Society for Nautical Research (Stowell House, New Pond Hill, Cross in Hand, Heathfield, East Sussex TN21 0LX), and the *Journal of Maritime Archaeology*, obtainable from Dr Jonathan Adams, Centre for Maritime Archaeology, University of Southampton, Southampton SO17 1BJ. For nautical terminology see F. H. Burgess's *Dictionary of Sailing* (Penguin, 1968), and for a glimpse of life under sail in the coastal trade see two books by Edmund Eglinton: *Last of the Sailing Coasters* (HMSO, 1982) and *The Mary Fletcher* (University of Exeter Press, 1990). For the archaeological and historical background to voyaging in the early north-east Atlantic see B. Cunliffe's *Facing the Ocean* (Oxford University Press, 2001).

Below is a selection of publications specific to the themes covered in this book.

Early water transport
Worldwide
Greenhill, B. *Archaeology of Boats and Ships*. Conway Maritime Press, 1995.
Johnstone, P. *Seacraft of Prehistory*. Routledge, 2001.
McGrail, S. *Boats of the World*. Oxford University Press, 2004.

The Americas
Bass, G. F. *Ships and Shipwrecks of the Americas*. Thames & Hudson, 1988.

Egypt
Jones, D. *Boats*. British Museum Press, 1995.
Landström, B. *Ships of the Pharaohs*. Doubleday, 1970.
Vinson, S. *Egyptian Boats and Ships*. Shire Egyptology, 1994.

Indian Ocean
Casson, L. *Periplus Maris Erythraei*. Princeton University Press, 1989.
Deloche, J. *Transport and Communications in India: Volume 2*. Oxford University Press, 1994.

Mediterranean

Casson, L. *Ships and Seamanship in the Ancient World*. Princeton University Press, 1986.

Morrison, J.; Coates, J. F.; and Rankov, N. B. *Athenian Trireme*. Cambridge University Press, second edition 2000.

Parker, A. J. *Ancient Shipwrecks of the Mediterranean*. British Archaeological Reports, S.580, 1992.

Wachsmann, S. *Seagoing Ships and Seamanship in the Bronze Age Levant*. Chatham Publishing, 1998.

Ethnographic rafts and boats

Greenhill, B. *Boats and Boatmen of Pakistan*. David & Charles, 1971.

Hornell, J. *Water Transport*. David & Charles, 1970.

McGrail, S. *Boats of South Asia*. Routledge Curzon, 2003.

Parry, M. H. (editor). *Dictionary of the World's Watercraft*. Mariners' Museum, Newport News, 2000.

Boatbuilding techniques

McGrail, S. *Ancient Boats in North-west Europe*. Longman, 1998.

Steffy, J. R. *Wooden Shipbuilding and the Interpretation of Shipwrecks*. Texas A & M University Press, 1994.

Navigation and pilotage

Lewis, D. *We the Navigators*. University of Hawaii Press, second edition 1992.

McGrail, S. 'Cross-Channel seamanship and navigation in the late-first millennium BC', *Oxford Journal of Archaeology*, 2. 3 (1983), 299–335.

Taylor, E. G. R. *Haven-Finding Art*. Hollis & Carter, 1971.

Excavation reports

Bruce-Mitford, R. *Sutton Hoo Ship Burial: Volume 1*. British Museum Press, 1975.

Crumlin-Pedersen, O., and Olsen, O. *Skuldelev Ships: Volume 1*. Viking Ship Museum, Roskilde, 2002.

Nayling, N., and McGrail, S. *Barland's Farm Romano-Celtic Boat*. CBA, Research Report 138, 2005.

Wright, E. *Ferriby Boats*. Routledge, 1990.

Index

Page numbers in italic refer to illustrations.